THE
MAN TX

THE

MANT💋X

LISA JAY

SHE IS WORTH FAR MORE THAN RUBIES AND PEARLS

Proverbs 31:10

A woman's guide to dating

LISA JAY

THE MANT❤X

Dedication

I dedicate this book to three incredible women who have made an impact on my life.

Many thanks to my rock, the one who inspired me, gave me strength and supported my every step throughout this wonderful journey of life.
- My Amazing Mother.

To my amazing sister, the only person in the world who knows me best, the one who has always been there for me and protected me.
You're one of a kind, thank you.

To a wonderful soul, the one who planted the seed that inspired me to write.
Michelle, this book is for you!

THE MANTOX
by Lisa Jay

The information contained in this book is general dating advice intended
to be educational. The material in this book should not replace
consultation with a medical professional.

LIBRARY OF CONGRESS CATALOGING-IN-PUBLICATION
DATA
JAY, LISA.
THE MANTOX/LISA JAY

66

Put on some red lipstick and
live a little.

-Unknown

CONTENTS

INTRODUCTION

When we think of detoxing, we think of cleansing and eliminating the toxins from our systems in order to make us feel like we're on top of the world again — right?

The Mantox is all about fresh starts. The positive changes you want to incorporate into your life can actually be achieved by making small adjustments to how you think. And today is the day to make those changes. Cleanse the negative self-talk out of your mind... Done? Perfect! Now we can get started.

If you're continuously finding yourself in difficult situations, attracting the same douchebags, experiencing mixed signals, and feeling a little confused — which leaves you wondering whether he is into you or if you're just wasting your time — you're not alone.

All these questions can drive a person mad, and by the end of it you've probably begun to doubt yourself. Your insecurities have kicked in and left you thinking that maybe there is something seriously wrong with you, because you can't seem to keep a man for longer than a month. After many failed dates and disappointments, some of you may lose hope, continue to blame yourself or give up on relationships altogether. Oh, the joys of #MEN, and the effects they have on us. They are both the cause and the cure to most of our problems!

Not to worry ladies, your fairy godmother is here! I've put together a guide to help you as you embark on your dating journey. Throughout this book, I will be sharing some of my personal encounters, along with a helpful guide on how to deal with certain situations — because let's face it, you wouldn't be turning to a self-help guide if you didn't need a little guidance.

Find out how to steer clear of Mr. Wrong, Mr. Time-waster and Mr. Good for nothing, and how to keep your eyes peeled for Mr. Right (and keep him wrapped around your little finger).

YOU ARE ALTOGETHER BEAUTIFUL, MY DARLING; THERE IS NO FLAW IN YOU.

Song of Solomon 4:7

It is not fancy hair, gold jewelry, or fine clothes that should make you beautiful. No, your beauty should come from within you - the beauty of a gentle and quiet spirit. That beauty will never disappear.

1 Peter 3:3-4

LOVE YOURSELF FIRST

First things first... YOU!
You only have one life, and it's in your hands, meaning that you get to create the life you want. However, figuring out what we want can be tough.

Happiness... it's what we are all seeking, right? We want to be happy in everything that we do. We want to be happy in love, not miserable. And if you aren't happy with yourself, you won't find happiness in a relationship. Happiness and love begin with you.

Over the course of this chapter, I will cover three stages to help you improve your life, and in turn, your relationships too.

Stage One – Love yourself!

"To love oneself is the beginning of a lifelong romance ."

- Oscar Wilde

Ladies, how on earth do you expect someone to love and value you if you can't even do so yourself? How can you expect a man — or anyone else, for that matter — to treat you like a diamond, or to put you on a pedestal if you don't believe you're worth it?

Learning to love and accept yourself is extremely important. In fact, doing so will allow you to let go of any insecurities that may cause you to limit yourself, devalue yourself and cause major problems in your relationships.

Society, furthermore, plays a huge part in making us feel like we aren't good enough, pretty enough, smart enough or skinny enough. This often leads us to believe that we've all got to look, dress and act in a certain way to be deemed acceptable. If you pick up a magazine, turn on the TV or flick through your news feed on social media, I'm sure you will stumble across many photoshopped images of what society considers 'perfection,' from flawless complexions, rocking bodies and other materialistic things. Sometimes it seems as though you can't escape from it all, and if you don't have these things, or if you're unable to meet these standards, then you are flawed. News flash! There is no such thing as perfection, we all have flaws and we all make mistakes. The opinion of others should never define who you are. In fact, if you allow others to define who you are, you are only giving them the authority to dictate your path.

You don't need to seek validation from others in order to feel good about yourself. The importance of high self-esteem — of self-worth — should already be instilled in your mind. You need to know and believe that you are good enough… You're more than good, actually! You are a unique individual, and it's time you celebrated your individuality. Be proud of who you are!
Learn to love, accept and value yourself! When you know what you are worth, you'll become more aware of what you deserve. And therefore, if you ever stumble upon someone who doesn't appreciate, respect or recognize your value, you are then more readily able to let it go.

You, my darling, deserve happiness; you deserve to love, and to be loved in return. YOU ARE WORTH IT!

Be careful what you think, because your thoughts run your life.

Proverbs 4:23

Stage Two – Change the way you think!

"Change your thoughts and you will
change your world."

– Norman Vincent Peale.

Did you know that your thoughts have the power to shape your life? Yes, your thoughts have the power to alter your future! However, YOU are the one who has the power to control the way you think. If you want to feel good and attract amazing people, then you need to train your mind to think in a certain way.

Your emotions affect the way you think, so the best way to control your thoughts is by controlling your emotions. It's really quite simple: When you feel good, you send out positive vibes, and when you feel down and depressed, you send out negative vibes. Your vibe attracts your tribe!

The moment you begin to think negatively, you will not only feel negative, but also attract negativity into your life. Dwelling on a negative thought will only bring about more negative thoughts, and that's when we get stuck in a rut. A positive life requires a positive mind, so change your thoughts in order to change your life. Your thoughts really do run your life. And let's face it, having a *positive attitude* in not always easy. You're bound to have crap days every so often, but the sun doesn't stop shining just because you've had a bad day. My number one rule is to give myself some time to dwell on the tough stuff, but only for thirty minutes — after that, it's time to stop feeling sorry for myself. If you notice you're feeling a little down, and you can't seem to snap out of your mood, listen to music, watch a comedy, go for a walk or trick your mind into believing that you are happy by smiling for two minutes. Trust me — you will instantly feel happier.

Release those endorphins, ladies. Doing so will put you in a much better mood. Dark chocolate helps me… in moderation, of course! *"Oh, who am I kidding? Sometimes I eat the whole block."* Find something that makes you feel good. It could be meeting a friend for a coffee, getting lost in a book, or killing it at the gym (I envy you ladies! I need serious motivation to go the gym.) De-cluttering is yet another way to change your mood, and it's actually quite cleansing. Throw out unnecessary junk; you will feel much better.

I like putting on some red lipstick, which makes me feel like I can conquer the world. Seriously, red lipstick and red wine makes me feel fabulous.

Stage Three – Be unapologetically you!

"Self-confidence is the best outfit, rock it and own it!"

- Unknown

#GETYOURSEXYON
That's right, you sexy thangs! Get your sexy on — and by this, I am referring to confidence.

I am by no means perfect. AH-MAZ-ING, yes; perfect, no... Do you see what I just did there? It's all about self-confidence. Let me start by telling you that I, like many others, have had self-doubt, self-image issues and at some stages I have hated and doubted myself. It's absolutely normal to feel like this; after all, we are only human, right?

We can be our own worst critic. Don't be so hard on yourself. Imperfections are what make you unique and beautiful. I want to stress how important it is to learn to love yourself, because loving and accepting yourself, flaws and all, will boost your confidence. Once you're entirely content with yourself, you will have nothing to hide or shy away from. You'll accept yourself for who you are, and once this happens it will reflect in your personality. This, my friend, is how confidence is born — by accepting who you are.

Confidence is like putting on a pair of high heels. As soon as you put on a pair of high heels, you feel unstoppable, your posture improves, you're standing tall, you're walking differently and you automatically feel sexier.

We notice confidence in men, and men most certainly notice it in women.

There's nothing more attractive than a person with confidence, because believing and knowing you are sexy is sexy!

You don't need to have a supermodel figure to be confident — confidence shows in the way you move, the way you speak and the way you carry yourself. However, you don't want to be overconfident, as that often translates into coming across as stuck up and unapproachable. Remain humble, get your head out of the clouds and come back down to reality. Having a superior attitude can be very intimidating for men, and they will find it extremely difficult to approach you.

When you are confident, you are like honey to the bees. I experienced this with my barista. I was extremely drawn to his amazing, confident personality. I found myself drinking about five espressos each day, just to get my daily dose of him. Crazy, right? Once again, confidence does play a huge part in attraction. Physically, he wasn't even my type, it was the way he moved, spoke and handled himself — he wasn't cocky, he was just confident. Don't confuse the two.

Now, you might be someone that finds it very difficult to be confident, or perhaps you are very reserved and quiet. You are not alone! As a child, I was an extremely shy girl, scared of the world. Who would have thought?

Yes, I too struggled to come out of my shell. It took me quite awhile to find myself. I was the girl who hid behind her mother's leg whilst being introduced to new faces. However, I found that surrounding myself with strong, positive and confident personalities really helped me to grow, and brought out traits in me that I didn't know existed.

Our journey through life is all about learning and growing, so there is no need to panic if you're not quite at that stage. It takes baby steps, and just like a butterfly, it requires time to evolve into the beautiful creature that you are meant to be. Don't be afraid of change! There is no reason to shy away from this big, beautiful world we live in. Be completely comfortable with yourself; surround yourself with confident, positive people, because their positivity will rub off on you. And most importantly, make sure to wear your confidence like a pair of heels — stand tall!

SHE IS CLOTHED IN
STRENGTH AND DIGNITY,
AND SHE LAUGHS WITHOUT
FEAR OF THE FUTURE.

Proverbs 31:25

LIVE, LEARN & MOVE FORWARD

Someone once told me that the universe will continue throwing life lessons our way until we actually learn our lesson. Let's take a moment to think about that for just a second. It makes perfect sense, and mistakes are not necessarily a bad thing, as each one offers a unique learning experience. However, it puzzles me when we don't apply the same method to our romantic lives.

Let's compare this to driving: You are happily driving along when you accidentally turn onto the wrong street. From that one wrong turn, we now know that we are heading in the wrong direction; but from making this slight mistake, we become more aware and familiar with that particular street, and so we avoid it because we know it's the wrong way. You wouldn't waste your time and turn onto the street just to get lost again, would you? No! Well, it's the same with men — you can't possibly expect a different result if you're heading in the same direction as always.

Let's say you meet a guy. Although he may seem like 'Mr. Wonderful,' you soon realize that he has very similar traits to the previous guy you dated — and that led to nothing but heartache. You decide to give it a go anyway, and then it fails. You are left upset and heartbroken; you start to whine and complain that men are all the same, and you can't really figure out why you're attracting the same men all the time. It can really start to feel like a cycle, and it can get quite frustrating.

So tell me, why on earth would you continue going in the same direction, only to get the same results? You've taken that path before, and it made you unhappy and miserable. Why not avoid it completely?

Your mistakes are meant for learning, not repeating! If you are attracting the same losers into your life as you were in the past, it's only because you have given them the key to do so. All experiences should be seen as learning lessons. Knowing, accepting and understanding your experiences, furthermore, will help you become more aware of what exactly you need to avoid. Only then will you know what you want in a man, and more importantly, what you deserve.

In your new guy, if you happen to notice even the slightest resemblance to your previous guy, then hit the road running. Run far away, and don't you ever look back. Ultimately, Mr. Wrong will give you a window of opportunity to recognize and welcome Mr. Right.

I will now reflect on my first relationship: I definitely learned a lesson from the experience, for which I am grateful. I have learnt that in order to maintain a successful relationship, that relationship needs to be built on a solid foundation of loyalty, trust and respect. Love, attraction and emotions are simply not enough for a relationship to weather the storm.

I know now I am not going to settle for the guy with the biggest smile, or the biggest wallet, and love will not overpower me, because I have already beat it once. I want it all or I want nothing! Moreover, trust should always accompany love, although my first relationship was definitely lacking in the matter. I was left feeling on edge all the time as the result of a constant stream of lies from him. In turn, I became very insecure, constantly questioning my ex's whereabouts, as I never knew whether he was out cheating or doing other pathetic things with his friends. After being in the dark, the uncertainty was enough to drive anyone crazy. My stomach was churning all the time, which resulted in petty arguments, ultimately ended with heartbreak.

I met him at work. It was my first day at my new job, and I entered the office to meet my new boss for the very first time. He was facing the other way, which meant his back was towards me whilst working on his laptop. I kindly interrupted him so I could introduce myself. As he turned around to greet me, we locked eyes for a few seconds, and then he nearly fell off his chair. At this point, I wanted to burst into laughter. However, I tried so hard to contain myself that, as expected, holding my laughter in created a build-up that left me laughing a lot louder than usual. AWKWARD! Did I make my boss weak in the knees? And did I just laugh in his face?

The new role I had just commenced meant the two would spend the entire day close enough to hear each other think. In time, we became good friends; our personalities were very similar, which helped the working day fly by.

After some time, however, I started to notice unusual behavior coming from my boss. I received phone calls from him on my days off from work, which he'd ask insignificant 'work-related' questions; and then, all of a sudden he treated me differently than the other employees. He snipped off his 'Tarzan' hairstyle, since he knew I despised it. A client, in fact, had even asked whether we were dating, as she saw the way he'd look at me, interested, and with puppy dog eyes. It soon became clear that my employer was attracted to me. Admittedly, I found myself talking about him all the time, too, with everyone — he was all I seemed to talk about with family and friends. Our feelings for each other were mutual. Yes, I fell in love with my boss. It happens! There was no way we could pursue a relationship, though, because that would have just been wrong. Unfortunately, once emotions are involved, you lose your sensibility. You cannot just flick love on and off like a switch; it just hits with no warning, and definitely without any confirmation needed. In other words, instead of listening to my brain, I followed my heart.

I was young and in love. Three years felt like ten years, and just like any ordinary couple, we fought like cats and dogs; we would break up and we would make up. It felt like we were a married couple: I was so comfortable with him that I was okay putting up with his crap. It turned out that all of his friends were single and he felt like he was missing out on 'The Single Life,' which was when he started to lie. Naturally, this would cause unnecessary arguments before the weekend, which would result in us not speaking from Friday through Sunday; and as soon as Monday came around, he would apologize. It became a cyclical pattern, but I continued to forgive him and allow him back into my life, because... well... I loved him. I put all my time and effort in trying to mend our broken relationship. I continued to hope that he would change. He continued to tell me he would 'change,' but that only ever lasted for a week or two. I was naïve, of course, and I believed him. However, what I didn't realize then was that you can't change people if they don't want to change themselves. Change comes from within.

As time went on, our arguments got worse, my frustrations grew, and I became very miserable. The happy, bubbly person that I once was had turned into the complete opposite. I wasn't myself; I was weak, and when I thought I'd gained the strength to walk away, his mind games would kick in, and once again I'd believe him and stay. He was like family to me — what would I do without him?

I became an emotional wreck, and I started to suffer from anxiety. There were times I found it difficult to breathe, and I found myself crying and unable to control my emotions more often than not. Then, one day I found I was all cried out. Seriously, I actually couldn't cry anymore; no tears would fall from my eyes, and it was like my emotions had just shut down. The pain overpowered all of the good memories, and I no longer felt anything for him. I quit my job and broke up with him on the same day, and I never looked back. This was undoubtedly one of the most difficult — but best — decisions I have ever made. I finally accepted that we were broken, and that no matter how many times I tried to glue our broken pieces back together, things would never be the same.

I held a grudge against him for many years, but that only created a blockage of which I needed to let go in order to trust other men again. It took some time, but eventually I forgave him and only then was I able to put the past behind me. We now remain friends, and we both realize we are better off friends than lovers.

Just remember that after every storm comes a rainbow! Yes, something very positive came from this situation. I am now a much stronger person, and I find that I am more selective with those in whom I choose to invest my time. I have met some amazing men in the wake of my breakup, and this is because I now know exactly what I want and what I deserve; I see my worth, and if I stumble across someone that isn't right for me, I no longer have any trouble saying goodbye. I've learnt that once you see your self-worth, you gain the strength to walk away from anything that no longer benefits you.

The more you learn, the more you'll grow, and the better you will become. Remember that each and every one of our choices creates experiences, both good and bad. These experiences are here to teach us, and lead us in the right direction.

Sometimes it takes a painful situation to make us change our ways.

Proverbs 20:30

"

Be careful of your thoughts,
for your thoughts become your
words.
Be careful of your words,
for your words become your
actions.
Be careful of your actions,
for your actions become your
habits.
Be careful of your habits,
for your habits become your
character.
Be careful of your character,
for your character becomes your
destiny.

- Lao Tzu

THE LIST

I bet you're thinking, what the heck is this so-called 'List'?

I am a huge believer in the laws of attraction: What you put out into the universe, you will attract into your own life. You have the power to attract anything you want into your life, and it all starts with your thoughts. You really have to feel it, and visualize it on a regular basis; it takes as little as five minutes a day. To successfully attract what you want, you need to know exactly what it is that you desire. The key is to focus on what you want rather than on what you don't want.

Trying to stay positive all day everyday can actually be quite difficult, but if you keep at it and train your mind, it will eventually become routine. Now, for those of you who do not know anything about the laws of attraction, I highly recommend that you do your research to gain a much better understanding of the matter, so then you can apply it to your everyday life. I suggest reading a book called 'The

Secret' by Rhonda Byrne. It's one of my favorites, as it explains everything you need to know about the powerful laws of attraction.

I decided to list all of the qualities that I wanted in a man. I wrote this list to remind myself of what I deserve, and more importantly, of the type of man I wanted to attract.

Lisa's List

* Good sense of humour
* Family-oriented
* Positive
* Affectionate
* Motivated
* Intellectual
* Loves sushi
* Loves to travel

Note: Notice how I have only written positive points. I didn't write negative qualities like, *no short men, no negativity, doesn't have bad breath*, etc. (Remember: You will only attract whatever you are focusing on.) Make sure to focus on the positive points rather than the negative ones. It is very important to watch your words.

My list started to get longer and longer, and it became ridiculous. Every morning on the train ride to work I would view my lovely, long list — and by view, I mean that I would visualize each and every point.

I remember chatting about the list with a friend of mine. As I was going through all the points, she stopped me halfway through and asked, "Lisa, you do know men like this only exist in a book of fairytales?" *Hmmm, I guess they do, I thought. Perhaps, I really do live in a fairytale land in my own mind.* But then I realized that hey, why should I settle for less? I am so content with myself, and I need somebody who will bring out the best in me, or compliment me. I want a lover, a life partner and most importantly, a friend — someone I can connect with and have fun with. Common interests are very important to me in my relationships. If a man doesn't like to travel, for example, that's a huge issue for me, and it's simply not going to work out.

Her comments didn't stop me from visualizing my perfect man, though.

About three months after our conversation, I met Prince Charming. He was a tall, handsome guy with a genuine heart and an amazing personality. And yes, he ticked each and every single box on my so-called 'unrealistic list'!

I was shocked! *Wow*, what more could I ask for? We went on incredible dates and had some amazing times together. In fact, each time we were out, he seemed to capture the attention of most straight women and gay men, and yet I always had his undivided attention, and he always made me feel like I was the only woman in the room. The only issue was that Prince Charming and I were at two completely different stages in our lives; we were like chalk and cheese. He wanted to settle down and have a more stable life, while I wanted to explore the big beautiful world. I had plans of opening my own bridal boutique, so marriage and a family were hardly at the top of my list of priorities at that particular moment in time. So we went our separate ways, and we both got what we wanted: He is now married, and I opened up my bridal boutique and continued to travel.

Now I do believe that you should make every new relationship an upgrade, but how can a person upgrade from Prince Charming? He was the whole package, with good looks, an amazing personality and a heart of gold. *Easy*, I said to myself. *Now I need a king*! A king would definitely be an upgrade, and so I began amending my list by erasing some old points and adding some new ones. I remember how much my mother and I laughed about my new list. If you thought for a second that my first list was unrealistic, then you can imagine what the new one looked like.

Forget Mr. Perfect — I was going to attract Mr. Incredible; I was upgrading to a king, and sure enough, I met one. Okay, not quite a king, but a lord. No, seriously. A lord. Like, a real-life lord. What were the chances? I guess it's true when they say *be careful what you wi-*

wish for. The laws of attraction are so powerful! Regardless of his title, this man truly was the ultimate upgrade from Prince Charming.

He was an absolute gentleman with an amazing English accent; his presence alone was enough to make any woman weak in the knees. He was very smooth in the way he spoke and carried himself; he dressed to the nines, and everything about him was intriguing and left me wanting more. I was truly captivated by him, from our very first conversation. We met whilst I was traveling, and just as I was about to leave the hotel, we magically crossed paths. I was very drawn to his charismatic personality; we had chemistry, an instant connection, that led to a long amazing conversation. However, it was getting extremely late, and just like Cinderella, I needed to go. I had to be up extra early the following day, but before saying our goodbyes, he invited me to have breakfast with him in the morning. I took his business card and said I would call him.

Rise and shine! Oh my, look at the time... I had overslept and, therefore, stood the man of my dreams up for breakfast. Whoops! I was also running extremely late, and all I could think about was getting to the port on time to sail off to the

Bahamas. I was going to be in the middle of the ocean for one whole week with absolutely no cell reception, and a very poor Wi-Fi connection. I couldn't get in contact with him even if I tried, and the only details he knew of me were the basics; my name, the country I live in and what I did for a living.

Well, never underestimate a man on a mission, because that was more than enough information for him to find me.

One week later I received a phone call from one of my employees, saying that a man from the UK has been trying to reach me. I was speechless! I mean, he didn't even have any of my contact details. Jeez, I must have made quite an impression for him to search for me like that. I eventually made contact with him; we spoke on the phone and continued to stay in touch with each other. Three days later, two hundred long-stem red roses appeared in my hotel room. He had sent them from the city where we met. A true romantic! Smooth, real smooth! *Could this man get any more amazing?* I wondered. *What am I to do with this big, beautiful bunch of roses?* I couldn't exactly take them on the flight back home with me. Instead, I decided to pull them apart and sleep in a bed full of rose petals... Two hundred roses, destroyed!

Months passed, but we remained in contact on a daily basis. However, as time went by, we drifted apart — not being able to see each other in the flesh made it easy forget about the strong connection we shared. We both had businesses to run, so it wouldn't have been easy to just pack up and leave.

A few months later, I eventually made my way to the UK to visit a good friend of mine, and since I was going to be in the same city as my London lover, I decided that it was only right to catch up with him. The day had finally arrived, and I wasn't at all nervous, because I had forgotten what it felt like to be around him. But as soon as I saw him... For the very first time in months, the feeling came crashing down like a ton of bricks. The connection, the sparks and the attraction were still there. Oh, WOW! I couldn't keep my eyes off of him, and by the look in his eyes, I knew that he was feeling exactly the same way. I mean, really — what's not to love about him? He was an amazing man, and did I mention that he was a fellow sushi lover? We were a match made in heaven!

We spent most of our time together, and grew closer and closer each day. I just felt so incredibly relaxed and comfortable around him; he felt like home, and when something feels like home, you don't ever want to part with it because it feels so right.

Emotions ran high the day of my departure, as my heart wanted to stay but my mind proved stubborn. I wasn't ready to leave, but my life, family and friends were all in another country; and on top of that, I had a business to run. I didn't want all of my time, effort and hard work to go down the drain, just because my heart was weak. Besides, what if it didn't work out? I was torn between two very different worlds, reality and love. My mind filled up with fear and doubt, and I couldn't stop it from running wild. I guess I was trying to make myself feel better by having doubts, so that it would be easier to walk away. I tossed and turned the whole flight home, and was miserable and emotional. Where were all these emotions coming from? Was I in deeper than I'd thought?

A few weeks later, my lord surprised me by traveling to my part of the world. I was ecstatic and speechless — talk about moving mountains! Neither of us could deny our strong connection, but this was no 'Cinderella story,' because at some point we had to face reality. Neither of us was willing to compromise. Long distance was difficult, and this man had baggage — a lot of it. To save us both the heartache, I made a difficult decision that simply had to be done. It was time to let our relationship go. Once I finally did, I felt a huge weight lift off from me, and instantly I knew that I had made the right choice. We do get in touch with each other from time to time, and he still sends me roses with notes that say: "Thinking of you always." Such a true gentlemen! There is no doubt that he will always remain in my heart, and be the man that truly swept me off my feet.

Well, well, well... a touchy story, right? That's not the point! I wanted to give you some insight into my world, and a few examples of how writing a list — combined with your thoughts, emotions and the powerful laws of attraction — has really helped me to attract some amazing men. All you need to do is know what you want, and to focus your thoughts on the positive. Then all you have to do is leave it up to the universe, and let it work its wonders by sending you the love of your life. It's time to unlock your positive thoughts and allow them to run wild and free — doing so will open the door to endless possibilities, not to mention a much happier life. What are you waiting for? Write it down and visualize it daily because you have the power to attract the man of your dreams. Allow the universe to make glorious miracles.

Ask and it will be given to you; seek and you will find; knock and the door will be opened to you.

Matthew 7:7

We must show love through actions that are sincere, not through empty words.

———— ❀ —— ❀ —— ❀ —— ❀ —— ❀ ————

JOHN 3:18

ACTIONS SPEAK
LOUDER THAN WORDS

Men are really not that difficult to read. In fact, men are very transparent. Whether or not they have feelings for you, how they act on the outside will reflect how they feel on the inside. However, when you're emotionally invested, this is where it can get quite tricky, because even though he might be showing you how he feels, you may not be able to make a clear judgment, because our personal feelings don't always allow us to see as clearly as we would like. This makes everything seem much more complicated than it actually is, and it can leave us feeling frustrated and confused.

What you need to know is that men will show you how they feel through their actions. Pay close attention because actions speak louder than words. A man can be a sweet talker to get what he wants; he will tell you he loves you, that you're beautiful and that you're the apple of his eye — and a whole bunch of other BULL Sugar-Honey-Ice-Tea. However, if his actions don't reflect what he's saying, then HOUSTON, WE HAVE A PROBLEM!

I am going to run you through a scenario that I have encountered to give you a better understanding of the issue.

One night, whilst I was out to dinner with a friend of mine, we were approached by the owner of the establishment we were dining at. It was not unusual for a business owner to engage in smalltalk, though. In fact, these were normal signs of a guy just doing his job. The restaurant owner was very funny and extremely entertaining, so we continued to chat. Each time he laughed, he would lightly rub my shoulder or touch my forearm. He was showing signs of attraction through body language, and I misread those small signs for someone that was just a tactile person — a guy just being friendly rather than someone who was attracted to me. However, I did start to notice that all of his questions were directed at me, and the conversation started to feel like he was trying to figure me out. I didn't mind, however, because I am a sucker for a man with a great sense of humor.

It started to become as clear as crystal that he wasn't just a guy doing his job; he was a guy who was experiencing attraction. He continued to find excuses to go back and forth to our table to chat, and to ask more questions. That was when he started to tell me about himself, and about the plans he had for his businesses — basically babbling on and on, and talking himself up. Not in a bad way, though, but like he was trying to impress me.

I really love men that ask you out on a date, rather than for just your phone number, and this was exactly what he did. He asked me out for a friendly coffee and in my opinion, I think this is the best way to get a woman's number — it just makes the whole situation a little less awkward, and it doesn't make the man appear sleazy. Through his actions, he had shown me that he was willing to actually make an effort; and consequently, I agreed to make time for us to get to know each other.

A man that wants you is never too busy for you, even if he only gives you five minutes of his time. A man who's interested will make the effort; a man who is not interested won't waste his time. Notice the signs and stop making excuses for his actions.
Ladies, if a man is showing you that he does not care, then you're better off believing it! He isn't too busy, or too tired; and no, he hasn't lost his phone, and he sure as hell hasn't accidentally dropped it down the toilet.

Our emotions often get the better of us, although we have a tendency to try to convince ourselves otherwise, but it's time to face the cold, hard truth: If he has suddenly stopped texting you, or if your conversation has drifted into a thing of the past, and if you find him a little aloof and distant towards you, it's a clear sign that he's just not interested. However, if he happens to be texting you on the odd occasion, it's a good chance that he is either passing his time or stringing you along. Don't allow your emotions to overpower your judgment. There is no point wasting time when the feeling isn't mutual.

In fact, I had been in this situation before; I was unaware that I was being strung along, it happened to me a very long time ago. Thank goodness I wasn't in too deep! I can't say that I wasn't attracted to him, but I was still in the early stages of attraction, and that's why I can look back and laugh about it now.

We only saw each other for a few months; we went out on a couple of dates and we stayed connected through messages. He would text me every single day, but he never bothered calling me. At first I thought that he just wasn't all that comfortable speaking over the phone, so I decided not to confront him about it. His texts started coming in less and less often, but we still caught up each week in person. At this stage, I was a little confused. *Is this guy into me or not?* I wondered. I mean, he couldn't keep his lips off mine, so what the hell was the go with this guy? I was getting mixed signals and didn't really know where I stood with him.

One night we decided to grab a coffee. I was driving, and he was in the passenger seat. As I pulled into the café parking lot, he immediately ducked his head, like he was hiding away from someone. He literally looked like he had seen a ghost, and then he shouted, "Keep driving!" like if we had just committed a crime and had to make a quick getaway. This made me stop the car and turn to see who he was so desperately trying to avoid. It turned out that he was hiding from the other woman he'd been stringing along. Yes, he was stringing us both, and God knows how many other women. Deep down I'd already known that there was something seriously wrong with our relationship, otherwise I wouldn't have questioned it, nor would I have had all those doubts.

What I have learnt is that you shouldn't have to question where you stand in a relationship; you should already know exactly what position you hold. The honeymoon phase should be a joyous time in any new relationship, if he isn't making an effort in the beginning, he won't be making an effort later down the track. Remember what you deserve and let it go!

When we become emotionally invested in a relationship, this can cause us to become blind and therefore, it becomes very easy to overlook the signs that are right in front of our eyes. Sometimes what we really need to do is push our feelings aside and face the reality of a situation. Holding onto false hope with a time- waster will only lead to heartache.

If you're feeling confused, then take a minute to step out of the box. View the situation from another angle, because most of the time we struggle to see what other people see. If you are questioning the mixed signals that you're receiving from him, then chances are he is unsure of the relationship. If he is texting only once or twice a week to touch base with you, then he is most likely stringing you along; he is keeping you there just in case option one fails, which means that you, my friend, are option two.

Men like to play this little trick called 'mind games'. They can easily twist and turn the story to make you feel like it's all in your mind, when in reality he is just a liar. You are not a fool, so don't allow him to play you for one. Don't ever settle for someone who treats you like an option, since you deserve to be the priority — you deserve to be someone's number one. For anything less, close the door on the relationship and move on.

Now let's focus on the men who are into you. My mother always said that if a man wants you, he will continue to chase. Remember, a mother knows best!

STOP, LOOK, LISTEN! Once again, actions speak louder than words! Did you know that an eyebrow raise, consistent touching of his face and (of course, my favorite one of all) mimicking the other person's body language are all forms of attraction? Who knew? Who pays attention to this stuff? I can't possibly be the only one who had absolutely no idea, It wasn't until I took some time to research the matter — to really test it out — that I thought to myself, "*Wow this is fascinating.*" And now I can't help but analyze a man each time I go out on a date, because I find all this very intriguing.

I must admit, I caught myself mirroring a man to whom I was very much attracted to. I was having dinner with my date, and we were seated directly opposite each other. Each time he took a sip of his drink, I found myself taking a sip of mine, and using the same hand he did — like he was staring directly into a mirror at his own reflection. That was when I realized that once I had put my drink down, I had subconsciously mirrored his exact movement. It was ridiculous!

When a person is attracted to you, they will subconsciously mimic your movements and facial expressions. Monkey see, monkey do. Try testing it out: Cross your arms, lean towards him, cross your legs, scratch or tilt your head; and if he starts to mirror your actions, then it's very likely that he is into you.

Men tend to change the pitch in their voices with women whom they are attracted to. Listen to the tone of his voice while he is speaking to you. If a man is using a lower-pitch voice, it's a clear indication that he is attracted. After all, we don't use our 'seductive voice' for just anyone.

Body language is a reflection of what you are feeling on the inside. Pay close attention to his feet.

The feet never lie; feet point you into the direction you want to go, therefore if both feet are pointing in your direction, he wants to approach you. If his feet are pointed away from you then he is most likely not interested.

There are, however, other, more obvious signs of attraction, flirting being number one on the list. Then there are the series of text messages, overwhelming compliments, smiling for no apparent reason in your presence, grooming himself, allowing you to invade his personal space, or finding any excuse to touch you (in a harmless, non-sleazy way, that is.) It's not rocket science: He is into you.

66

No one acts more foolishly than a wise man in love.

- Unknown

"

Take a lover who looks at you
like maybe you are magic.

- Frida Kahlo

SIGNS OF ATTRACTION

Some men lack the tendency to express their emotions; and if that's the case, then how can you tell if a guy is into you? It's time to put an end to the questions once and for all. I find it's best to judge a man by his actions, so I've put together a list of things that men often do when they are attracted to you. A man that is interested in you will show a minimum of five signs. You can't possibly believe he is into you if he only displays one of these signs. If you have not experienced at least five of these signs on his behalf, then grab a pair of invisible scissors and cut all ties.

He calls:

Forget text messages — a man that's extremely into you will actually pick up the phone and call you. This is not because he wants to have a chat, but because he wants to hear your voice! The phone call does not have to be very long either, but if he is dialling your number, then there's no doubt about it: He is into you.

He will brag about himself:

This can make him appear a little conceited, but trust me when I say this: A man only brags and speaks highly of himself because he likes you and wants to impress you. Don't be surprised when he starts going on about his successes and accomplishments, how much money he earns, or how strong and awesome he is. He is just trying to prove that he is worthy of you!

Chivalrous gestures:

Chivalry is not dead when it comes to men who are attracted or in love. A man that adores you will express his affection through sweet gestures like opening the car door, pulling your chair out for you, offering you his coat in cold weather or picking up the bill on a date. Not only is he trying to impress you, but he is also trying to show you that he cares, and that he is very capable of taking care of you.

He asks a lot of questions:

Asking questions in an attempt to learn more about you is a sign of interest. You will find him wanting to know every single detail of your life, like you're being interviewed for the lead role of Farmer Wants a Wife. Can you cook? How many siblings do you have? What's your favorite food? Where's your favorite place to dine?

Showering you with romantic gifts:

No surprises here — if a man is buying you gifts (and it's not your birthday), then it's clear he is head over heels. Gifts show that he is thinking of you. It doesn't necessarily need to be the oh-so-typical chocolates, flowers, jewelry or perfume. He could surprise you with a cup of coffee, or send you love songs lyrics or a poem.

He makes physical contact:

If he is interested in you, you will notice more physical contact. He will find subtle ways to touch you, like pushing your hair away from your face, brushing against your arm, patting you on the back or touching your hand. Physical contact is a clear sign that he really likes you.

Holds your hand:

Holding hands in public indicates that he is proud to show you off to the world, and that he wants everyone to know that you are a couple. When there are other men around, you will find him reaching for your hand, or he will most likely put his arm around your waist or shoulder, making it clear that you are his. In other words, you're taken, so other men should back off!

Admiring you:
You will often catch him smiling or gazing at you like he's under your spell; a man that stares at you without saying a word is clearly attracted, and most likely infatuated, especially when he can't wipe that grin off his face in your presence.

Grips you tightly:
If he hasn't said the three magic words yet, then be prepared. If a man hugs you tightly, it's a sign that he does not want to let you go, and if he squeezes your hand tightly and kisses it, he is already communicating that he loves you.

All eyes on you:
There could be go-go dancers wearing nothing but feathers and sparkles. However, if a man is giving

you his undivided attention, even with other women in the room, then he is smitten by you. By the looks of things, you are the apple of his eye.

He will get jealous:

What's mine is mine, right? We all get a little territorial when we develop feelings for someone. Men are no different — if he is interested, he will most likely get jealous when you talk about a male friend, or when you are around other males.

Includes you in his future plans and decision making:

Do you find him including you in his future plans? Whether you're a plus-one at an event or planning a vacation six months in advance, including you in his future plans means he sees you in his future, and believes that the relationship will last. You might find him asking you for your input when making decisions; it could be something as simple as choosing which sofa to buy, or selecting the design of his new business cards — a man that does this truly values your opinion.

He gets protective of you:

Men have a tendency to be protectors, especially when it involves the women they care about. Your man wants you to feel safe and secure in his presence. You might notice this when you're walking along the outer path of the sidewalk — he will switch positions with you so that you are out of harm's way; he will walk you to your car, or if you are traveling through a crowded place, he'll take hold of your hand and lead the way. Like a knight in shining armor, he's there to save the day.

He finds any excuse to be around you:

A man that's extremely interested in you is like a little puppy that's craving your love and attention. If he could, he would probably pounce on you with excitement and lick your face. He just wants to be around you — to be in your presence all the time — and so he will find excuses to get his daily dose of you. Did you say your car needs repairs? Or that a lightbulb needs replacing? The next thing you know, surprise, surprise! All of a sudden, he has become a master of all trades.

If he opens up to you:

Remember that trust is earned, so if he is revealing

his deepest thoughts, feelings and experiences, then he trusts you and feels comfortable around you. He wants to connect with you, so if you find him saying something like, "I've never told anyone that before," or "You're the first person I've said this to," then he is opening up his big bag of secrets and letting you in. He wants you, and for you to know more about him.

He notices the little things:

If you were to wear the same piece of jewelry every single day, and then happened to take it off, wait for him to immediately point it out. Even our close friends and family don't take notice of this stuff! So when you think he is not paying attention, think again! Men tend to remember things you've said, and will pay close attention to details concerning the women they are attracted to.

He agrees with you:

When a man is in love, you are automatically thrown into the express lane of his heart, and your opinion matters — anything you say, goes. You think he should grow a beard? "Your wish is my command," he'll reply, and magically, the beard appears. Oh, but wait... Now you don't like it — and that's okay, because all of a sudden he doesn't like it either, and has booked an appointment at the barber shop.

"

Sweetheart, the right guy will make you a priority. If you find yourself feeling like you're not good enough, it's because he's not good enough.

- Steve Maraboli

"

Nothing worth having
comes easy.

-Unknown

THE LOVE GAME

What is the game you ask?

Some of you might already know about the game, some of you may not even be aware of the game, and some of you might be thinking I just don't have time for games. Whichever it may be I will explain a little more in-depth about the game and why every woman should be playing it.

Why is it that the men we are not attracted to always seem to text, call and continually ask us out for coffee?
I mean, really — did he not get the message that you were not interested? You brushed him off over 10 times by making up excuses whenever he asked you out for a coffee. You took your sweet time to respond to his texts, and when you did respond, you were very blunt or cold. Sometimes you pretended that you didn't even see his texts, and you ignore his calls in the hopes that he will eventually get the message that you're just not interested. You're hoping that eventually he'll just give up, but it seems as though no matter how ma-

ny times you've brushed him off, he will still try his luck and continues to chase you. We all know there's an easier option — just saying "I AM NOT INTERESTED!" — but you didn't want to be rude, because he's a really nice guy, and you wanted to let him down lightly, without being a heartbreaker. Fair call... although, he still thinks he has a chance, and you have just become ten times more attractive because, well... we all want what we can't have.

You, my darling, were unknowingly playing the game.

Yes, the game! Also referred to as 'Hard to Get' or 'The Chase,' and by the sound of things, you are a damn professional at it. You're hard to get, and you didn't even have to try. That's because showing a man you are not interested makes you a challenge, and we all know that men love a challenge.

I want you to rewind back to a time when you were interested in a guy; and think about how you responded. Chances are you were quick to drop everything and go out on that coffee date. He texts you, and you reply a minute later. You don't want the calls to end, so you yap on about anything and everything. You're there at the click of his fingers and before you know it, he has disappeared into thin air. No phone calls, no texts... NOTHING, not even a peep. *Why, oh why?* you ask. But I think you already know the answer... you were just too available.

It really is that simple... Men love women who play hard to get. Playing hard to get will make you appear mysterious and unpredictable, and men will thrive off getting your attention and trying to find out every single detail about you. You will notice more texting, more calls and more dates — with plenty of notice.

Game rules:

Note: Don't ever change the person you are — and this is not about personality. You don't need to become a major b*tch to prove that you are hard to get. Be authentically you!

1. He is the cat and you are the mouse. A mouse never chases the cat.

2. Presentation is everything! They say not to judge a book by its cover, but in this case your image and the way you present yourself says a lot about you. The way you dress can play a massive part in how the world perceives you.

If you're going to dress like trash, then know you'll likely be treated as such. Keeping it classy will never go out of fashion. There is nothing wrong with showing a little skin, but don't be too revealing, as this sends mixed messages, and in that case you will most likely attract the men that only want you for one thing. Ladies, if you are going to attract a man with your body, then they will only want you for your body. Try and keep things for the imagination — doing so is much more appealing.

3. When he sends you a text, do not reply straight away. This will keep him on his toes for awhile. Note: Responding to a text too soon shows that you are too keen.

4. When he ask you out on a date, it is so important that he gives you plenty of notice. You are an independent woman with a very busy schedule. Your time is valuable, and therefore, he needs to earn it. He needs to know that you are not going to drop everything just to spend time with him. This will make him work harder for your attention, and put him in the habit of giving you plenty of notice before each date. If he gives you less than 3 days' notice, you must kindly decline. He does not need to know the details — just say you've already made plans, or that you are busy that day.

5. When you're on a date, make sure it doesn't exceed a 4 to 5 hour timeframe. Remember, no more than 5 hours! You are a busy woman — you have things to do and people to see, and he isn't priority.

6. Don't be an open book. Allow him to get to know you in small doses. A mistake most women make on first dates is revealing too much too soon. If you don't leave some things unsaid, he will most likely lose interest.

7. Act like a lady! You are not one of 'the guys,' so if you want to be treated like a lady, you need to play the part right. Getting thrown into the friend zone is all to easy; and your aim is getting him to view you as a potential lover, and not just as 'the cool chick.'

8. Don't stick to him like glue. No one likes a clingy person; clinginess is annoying and unattractive. I mean, how is he ever going to miss you if you're always there?

9. Avoid talking about commitment, especially if you've only known him for a few weeks. If you're going to bring up the whole 'commitment talk' too soon, he will be running as far away from you as he can. I mean, really, commitment is a huge deal, enough to scare anyone away. This is a conversation for another time.

Note: Your aim is to make him fall head over heels at the beginning; and after you have succeeded in your quest, I can guarantee that he will be the one asking you to commit.

10. Don't sleep with him on the first date. You're a lady, so keep it classy. A man that really wants you will want to peel through each and every layer of your mind before getting into bed with you. He will respect you more if you wait.

POWER OF THE P

Our lady parts make women similar, but our minds make us unique. If you do not have his heart, then sex will never be more than sex; and before you know it, the power of the P has exceeded its time limit, and he's now on the hunt for the next best thing. So, if you think for a second that the power of the P will keep him around, think again! The power of the P may work for a married couple, or for couples that are head over heels for each other, but you, my darling, are not at that stage (at least not yet).

You want him around for a long time, and not just for a good time, especially if you're looking for something a little more serious. A woman who plays the game is not easy. A woman who plays the game knows her worth, and highly values herself and her body. And consequently, he doesn't get the opportunity to explore your body right away. After all, sex is almost always on a man's mind, and I'm sure that sex with you has crossed his mind more than a million times.

This is why I am urging you not to rush into sex right from the start. This can reveal quite a lot about a man's intentions. A man who takes the time to get to know you before sleeping with you is someone who has genuine feelings for you. Therefore, he will respect your decision and wait until you're ready.

A man that runs for the nearest exit because you didn't sleep with him on his schedule clearly wanted just one thing — your body! Don't you dare dwell on things because you've lost him. After all, why would you want a man who only wants you for sex? It's time to wake up because you are not a sex object. You want somebody that's going to respect you and your body.

Your body is your temple, your home; it's where your soul resides. We are only given one body, and it is our responsibility to take good care of it.

Above all else, gaurd your
heart, for everything you do
flows from it.

———— ••• —— ••• —— ••• —— ••• —— ••• —— ••• —— •••

Proverbs 4:23

FIRST DATE POINTERS

First impressions are everything! A first date is like an interview, so you need to put your best foot forward and make one hell of an impression.

* Make an effort with your appearance; remember that men notice the little things. Make sure your nails (including your toenails) are well manicured. Dress appropriately for the date, and don't be afraid to show a little skin — you want to walk into a room and turn heads. And I'm not just talking about your clothes, but also your scent. I know that personally, I am extremely drawn to men that smell good. A little perfume never killed anybody. I sure hope not, anyway — just don't overdo it.

* Don't try and be someone you are not; just be yourself (meaning the best version of yourself). Be happy, positive you! No whining or complaining, which makes the date awkward and you unattractive to the guy. And there should definitely be no ex-boyfriend talk — save it for your next gossip session with your girlfriends.

* There is no right or wrong way to have a conversation. However, don't be too revealing — there's no need to open up about every detail of your life. Keep it short and simple! Your aim is to keep him on his toes and wanting more of you.

* It's okay to flirt, since flirting shows that you are interested. Be cheeky, but don't dirty talk. Talking dirty can really give off the wrong impression, and before you know it, his only goal will be to try and get you into bed.

* Keep the date short, meaning 4 or 5 hours maximum! I don't care how much fun you are having — you must not exceed that time limit. A prize isn't just handed over on a silver platter; it is earned, and your man must earn his time with you.

* If he offers to pay at the end of the date, don't argue with him! I am sure he is well aware that you are fully capable of taking care of yourself, so stop trying to prove a point. Say thank you and pay for him another time (if things work out, that is). Some men feel uncomfortable letting women pay for anything; however, there are other ways to sh-

ow your appreciation. Prepare some snacks and drinks and take him out on a nice romantic picnic, or you can surprise him with a home-cooked dinner. If you are like me, and have absolutely zero cooking skills, then I highly suggest taking another route. Buy some Italian takeaway and pretend you made it… Wink, wink. I'm only joking — don't do that! It will bite you in the ass later down the road. Buy a pizza and his favorite drink and host a movie night for him!

NOTE: If a man has asked you out on a date, it is his responsibility to pick up the bill. This can be a deal breaker. If he hasn't got a brain, then he will suggest splitting the bill, or worse, making you pay for everything. It's not about being greedy — it's about him stepping up and being a gentleman.

* Don't contact him to say you had a great night. You already thanked him at the end of the date. Allow him do the chasing — if the date went well, then you'll definitely hear from him. It doesn't necessarily have to be that same night, so calm your knickers! When you do receive that text, make sure you remember not to reply immediately. Keep him guessing for a while.

If you have made it to the second round, and he is asking you out on a second date, congratulations! Make sure he gives you 3 to 4 days' notice — you should say no to anything less than that.

DON'T break the rules of the game!
And remember: The chase is always better than the catch, but anticipation is what makes us want something that much more.

"

Love yourself.
Forgive yourself.
Be true to yourself.

How you treat yourself sets the
standard for how others will
treat you.

- Steve Maraboli

Encourage one another and
build each other up.

Thessalonians 5:11

TIPS FOR A
SUCCESSFUL RELATIONSHIP

Don't disrespect your partner's family
Unfortunately, your relationship is not always going to be sunshine and rainbows. Things don't always pan out the way we'd like them to, and that big happy family you envisioned in your mind may very well turn out to be the crazy family from hell.

Not seeing eye to eye with your partner's family can put a strain on your relationship. However, you're not the victim here, your partner surely is! He will feel torn between you and his family; he will constantly feel the need to make an effort to keep both you and his fam-bam happy. There is no harm in telling him how they make you feel, but don't ever bad-mouth or disrespect your partner's family in the process. In fact, doing so will fail to solve any of your problems — it will only create more of them. Remember that you can't choose your family, and at the end of the day those people are, and always will be, your partner's family. And furthermore, family quarrels are none of your business! If he happens to be venting about his family, that does not give you the right to badmouth them too. You should support your partner by being a good listener, but please remember not to judge.

Be a team
You are a team, and being a team means that he represents you and that you represent him. You have the power to make or break each other. When you put your man down, you are putting yourself down as well. You should never disrespect or put your partner down, PERIOD!

Build him up, don't tear him down
There is no need to tear your partner down just because you're not on speaking terms. When you badmouth or brag about your significant other to your family and friends — especially regarding minor disagreements — you will only make him look bad. Family and friends will always side with the person whom they are closest to, and that person is you! It's very important to learn to keep your private life PRIVATE. You and your partner will eventually kiss and make up, but your family and friends will continue to resent him. And this, my friend, creates unnecessary problems.

Never show up empty-handed at family events

When your significant other invites you to family events, the last thing you want to do is show up empty-handed. You should always bring a gift when you're invited into someone else's home, especially if you're meeting you're meeting your partner's parents for the first time. Whether you choose to bring a bottle of champagne, chocolates or flowers, arriving with a small gift in hand is a great way to show your appreciation —and the person receiving the gift will be touched by the thoughtful gesture!

Avoid arguing in public

Don't ever argue or settle your disagreements in public. It's disrespectful, uncomfortable and will make both parties look like fools. The whole entire world — including your family and friends — does not need to know about your private life. There is a time and place for everything, which means you should always resolve your disagreements behind closed doors.

Don't ever stop dating

When you are in a long-term relationship, it's easy to get comfortable, and after awhile the excitement fades and the spark begins to disappear. Consequently, you must make it a habit to get up and go out on dates with your man — and this will require you dress up and look glamorous. These nights are all about you and your man, so avoid restaurants that have television screens, and switch your smartphones off.

Don't smother him
Don't suffocate your man with phone calls or text messages when he is out with his friends. He is not a child, and you are most certainly not his mother. Trust is important, and if you do not have trust in your relationship, then it's time to reevaluate it.

Quit Nagging and Complaining
Nagging, whining and complaining about petty things will suck the life out of your relationship. STOP RIGHT THERE! Think about what's more important, and learn to address the issue at hand with a positive attitude. If you continue to whine and complain, he will eventually learn to tune you out — or worse, you will push your man away.

Cook for him
Men like to feel nurtured, and a great way to nurt-

ure the person you love is to whip up a fantastic meal for him. After all, food makes the heart grow fonder, and the best way to a man's heart is through his stomach.

Kiss Often

Express your love through an intimate kiss, and see to it that you and your man kiss each other on a regular basis. I know many couples who become so comfortable around each other that they no longer feel the need to show affection. However, kissing is a form of bonding, and it's a great way to express your feelings without having to say a single word. Oh, and did I mention that kissing burns calories? It's a win-win situation!

Compliment him

Men love compliments just as much as women do. Everyone likes to be praised for their efforts, and compliments are a great way to show him that you appreciate what he does for you. Men thrive off attention and recognition, after all. Your opinion matters, and whenever you acknowledge something he does, you will most likely get more of it.

Give each other space

A major factor in maintaining a happy, successful relationship is respecting each other's privacy and giving each other space. As much as you enjoy spending quality time together, freedom and space are crucial to your relationship. Spending time apart (to an extent, of course) will allow your relationship to flourish, and the distance will make you miss each other immensely.

Never let yourself go

Just because you're in a relationship doesn't mean you should stop maintaining your appearance. It's okay to be comfortable, but don't ever get so comfortable that you begin to neglect yourself. Always make an effort to impress each other — making an effort to look good for your man will keep your relationship alive.

"

Happiness resides not in possessions, and not in gold, happiness dwells in the soul.

- Democritus

LOST IN LIMBO

Weeks have passed and things seem to be going pretty well — you are now receiving your regular *good morning* and *goodnight* texts. AWW! Conversation between the two of you has grown deep and effortless; you feel like you are walking on cloud nine, and that nothing can go wrong. *Life is amazing! Life is fabulous... Wait, what? Why hasn't he responded to my text?* One hour turns to two, and two turns to three; you're still waiting, and it's been six hours! *Okay, should I call? Maybe something happened to him? That can't be right, though. I just stalked him on social media and he was online a minute ago.* You've been waiting all day for a text back, and he finally decides to reply... 10 hours later! *Hallelujah!!!* Sound familiar?

For the men reading this, BEWARE! Because we are watching your every move. If we ask questions, then chances are we already know the answers to them. Tip: Tread carefully! Answer our questions wisely, truthfully and with extreme caution. And ladies, don't deny it! You and I both know that when it involves our man, we women are professional investigators. The FBI has nothing on us.

But hold your horses, ladies; take a deep breath and calm down. This is not uncommon. It is, however, unusual behaviour, and of course it's only natural to panic. What you are experiencing is called mixed signals, and yes, it's frustrating! You're left waiting in Limbo. Where do you stand? What to do? And where do you go from here?

Before you jump the gun and get all crazy and emotional, you need to keep in mind that we are only human, and that every individual processes things differently. There are going to be occasions where we all need a little time to clear our minds, and sometimes you need to allow your man to process whatever he might be going through in his own way, and at his own pace. Whether it's about doubting the relationship, work-related issues, problems at home or a disagreement you might have had in the recent pass, he will eventually open up when he is ready, so don't force it. Still, this doesn't change the fact that you're confused.

There is a seven-day rule you must follow in order to know where you stand; over these seven days, you are not to make any contact with your man unless he reaches out to you first. If he is backing off and distancing himself away from you, then it's obviously for a reason.

The seven-day period will show you how much he actually cares; and this could go two ways, since you either hear from him or you don't. Usually, by the third day, he is missing you and has realized that you have been distant, and so he will make contact regardless of what he's going through. Some men may need a little more time, and will most likely make contact with you by the seventh day. It is in a man's nature to go after what he wants, and if you haven't heard from him even after seven days, then it is clear that what he wants doesn't concern you.

Sometimes it could just be a misunderstanding — he thinks you're not interested, you think he's not interested, and then you both decide to back off... Bet you thought I was serious there for a second, since this is what most of us like to believe... Miscommunication!

The thing is, men already know what they want! If they want you, then my darling, you will know all about it. You shouldn't have to chase a relationship, but if you must test the waters to get some sort of closure, then be my guest. I suggest sending him a brief message just to touch base, and you'd better take note of how he responds. If he is quick to reply and wants to continue talking with you, then that's great news. If he is cold towards you, and responds back with a closed off message, then you've got your answer. And hopefully that answer can offer you closure. Don't bother getting all crazy with the questions about why things didn't work out between the two of you. You're probably not going to get an honest answer from him anyway, so don't waste your time on someone that doesn't have feelings for you. Yes, it's going to hurt, and you will feel disappointed, but holding on to false hope, and being led on, will only leave you heartbroken. Let it go, and do so without any grudges. Don't allow another person to turn you bitter; you have so much love to give, and you will find someone who will give you the same love in return. They will truly fit into your life, like the missing piece to the puzzle.

The beauty of life is that we have choices, and we get to be in control of them and decide what we want — what paths to take, and who will join us on our amazing journey through life. Being single should be your prime time to focus on bettering yourself, as there's always room for improvement. Be happy and content with yourself, and when you meet him, Mr Right will be an added bonus to your happiness. Your happiness should never be defined by an object or a person; it should come from within, and that's when you'll have everything to gain and nothing to lose.

There are billions of people on this earth, and it is only normal to stumble across Mr. Wrong, Mr. Timewaster and Mr. Player. However, this should never be an excuse to give up on the chance to find extraordinary love.

Good luck, ladies!

Love never fails.

Corinthians 13:8

Illustration by Olowek, an amazing artist from Poland. Thank you!

Lisa Jay was born and raised in
Sydney, Australia.
Lisa developed the desire to
inspire others after a painful
heartbreak that forced her to
make positive life changes. She
felt immense blessings for the
experiences she soon
encountered after making such
changes. In turn she felt driven
to share her knowledge, and
provide positive inspiration to
improve the lives of others.